Technology in the Time of
Ancient Greece

Judith Crosher

WAYLAND

Titles in the series

Ancient Egypt   **The Aztecs**

Ancient Greece   **The Maya**

Ancient Rome   **The Vikings**

Cover picture: Archimedes' screw, which was used to raise water from a river to irrigate crops.
Title page: A statue of a Greek god, found in the sea off southern Italy.

Book editor: Rosemary Ashley
Series editor: Alex Woolf
Designers: Sterling Associates
Illustrator: Tim Benké

First published in 1997 by
Wayland Publishers Ltd
61 Western Road, Hove
East Sussex, BN3 1JD

Find Wayland on the internet at http:/www.wayland.co.uk

British Library Cataloguing in Publication Data
Crosher, Judith
  Technology in the Time of the Ancient Greeks
  1. Technology–Greece–History–Juvenile literature
  2. Greece–Civilization–To 146 B.C.–Juvenile literature
  I. Title II. Ancient Greeks
  609.3 '8

ISBN 0 7502 2045 7

Typeset by Sterling Associates
Printed and bound by G. Canale & C.S.p.A., Turin

Contents

Introduction

In the third century BC, the ancient Greek philospher Anaximenes wrote, 'Poverty makes men cleverer and more skilled in the craft of life.' Greece was never a rich country and, because of this, its people had to develop new technology to help them make the best of their resources.

From other civilizations the Greeks inherited four basic technical devices for increasing muscle power: the lever, the wedge, the windlass and the pulley. Not only did they find new uses for these tools, they invented a fifth; the screw.

Between 400 and 391 BC Hippocrates founded the profession of physician or doctor – separating medicine from religion. He developed the Hippocratic Oath, which is still used by doctors today. Some years later, between 384 and 322 BC, Aristotle wrote a book in which he described the use of pulleys, wedges and levers. He asked qustions such as, 'Why, if you put an axe on a piece of wood with a heavy weight on the axe, it won't split the wood, but if you swing the axe, it will, even though the axe is lighter than the weight?'

The Parthenon, in Athens

This wonderful example of Greek architecture was built in the fifth century BC.

Between 260 and 241 BC Archimedes invented a screw-pump for raising water, (see page 7). He designed a crane to save the city of Syracuse from the Romans in 212 BC. When enemy ships sailed close to the city walls a hook was lowered; it caught on a ship's prow and lifted, capsizing the ship. He was once asked by the king of Syracuse to work out the proportion of gold and silver in a crown. To do that he had to find the exact volume of the crown without melting it down. Archimedes realized how to do this as he was getting into a full bath tub and observed how his body displaced a volume of water.

This book is about Greek craftspeople; the tools they used and the technology they developed, not only to produce their clothes and food, but to create their unique pottery, their beautiful statues and their amazing temples.

Ancient Greece

This map shows some of the most important towns and cities of mainland Greece, the Greek islands and neighbouring regions, at the height of the Ancient Greek civilization.

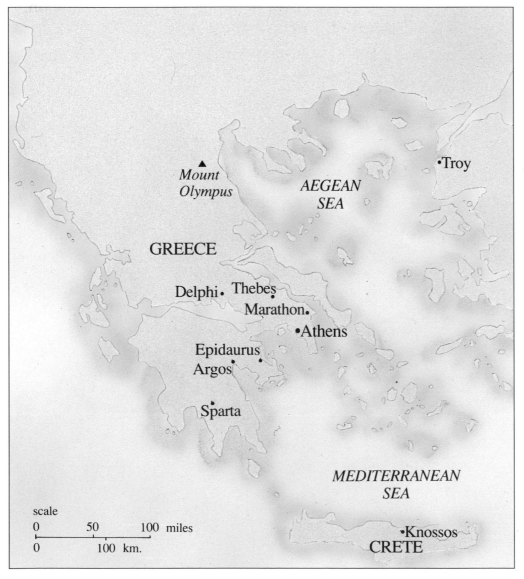

Farming

A Greek farmer worked hard to make a living from his dry, stony land. He had few animals to manure the soil, so he had to rest the soil for a year between crops. He sowed wheat and barley in autumn, to catch the winter rains. He scratched a furrow in the soil with his iron-tipped plough, drawn by oxen or mules, and his son or a slave walked behind, dropping seeds into the furrow.

With so little flat land there was no point in developing machines for cutting crops – the Greeks used the same design of hand sickles for hundreds of years. But they invented a single tool that could do two jobs. A lump of iron beaten into a spike on one side and a wide, flat blade on the other, fixed to a handle, could chop and root out tree stumps and dig holes. It was an essential tool for clearing the land for planting olives and grapevines.

Ploughing

This clay figure shows a man ploughing with two oxen. The plough dug a shallow furrow in the hard soil; it did not turn the soil over as modern ploughs do.

Vine dresser's knife

This was the Ancient Greek version of the Swiss Army knife. Its six sections each did a different job.

rostrum
for hollowing

scalpum
for smoothing

sinus
for cutting
and pulling

mucro
for clearing

securis
for hacking

culter
knife blade

Archimedean screw

The Archimedean screw drew water out of a stream or canal, raising it over a low bank and into the field. It is still used today.

How the Greeks made and used the Archimedean snail (screw)

1 First the carpenter made the shaft. He drew eight equally-spaced lines from one end to the other of a wooden pole, and lines around the pole, making a pattern of small squares all over it.

2 Next he painted a strip of willow with pitch and, starting at one end, nailed it around the shaft, each time crossing exactly where the lines met. It went round the shaft five times. This made the base of the first blade.

3 He built up the blade with more willow strips, making a giant screw.

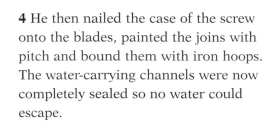

4 He then nailed the case of the screw onto the blades, painted the joins with pitch and bound them with iron hoops. The water-carrying channels were now completely sealed so no water could escape.

5 The screw was mounted on wooden posts. One end rested in the water. The other end, on the riverbank, was probably turned by pushing with the feet. As it turned, each blade picked up water and carried it far enough for the next blade to pick it up.

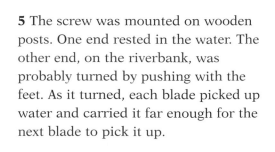

Preparing food

Grinding wheat

Housewives first ground wheat by putting handfuls of grains on a flat stone and rubbing them round and round or back and forward, with a smaller stone, using both hands.

One historian described the usual Greek dinner as: first course – a kind of porridge, second course – a kind of porridge. It was not quite as bad as that. Bread, lentils, barley and beans, cooked in different ways were the basis of every meal, but there was also goats' cheese, fish, fresh vegetables, honey, figs and grapes, olives, wine, and meat at festivals.

The basic foods – wheat, barley, grapes and olives – all needed hard work to turn them into flour, wine and oil. Gradually the Greeks developed machines to help them with the work, each one more efficient than the last.

A machine for grinding wheat

Then the Greeks invented a machine that could be worked using only one hand. It had two flat stones, the upper with a slit to pour in the grain, and a handle to push it from side to side. Later they invented the rotary mill, turned by a handle, which was easier than pushing from side to side.

Harvesting grapes

Grapes were picked and collected in baskets. The first stage of wine-making was to tread the grapes in stone basins. The leftover mush was piled into rings of twined grass on a table.

Pressing grapes

To press the grapes, farmers used a wooden beam fastened to the wall, weighted with stones – and workers. Later, they fixed a pulley turned by a windlass to the end of the beam, to make pressing easier. After the screw was invented, about 300 BC, they fixed a big wooden screw to the floor and through the end of the beam.

Crushing olives

Ripe olives were knocked off the trees and collected in baskets. Because olives are harder than grapes they were first put into a trapetum, a machine with two revolving millstones. The gap between the millstones and the sides and bottom of the trapetum was just wide enough to partly crush the flesh but not the bitter olive stones. The pulp was scooped out and pressed in a wine press. After pressing, the oil and juice were put in pottery jars so that the oil could float to the top.

Make a Cretan watercress salad

You need:
2 tbs of red wine vinegar, 1 tsp of honey, 2 tbs of currants, 4 cups of washed watercress, a quarter cup of chopped lovage leaves or a finely chopped celery stick, a quarter cup of olive oil, salt and pepper.

Heat the vinegar, honey and currants in a saucepan (not aluminium). Leave to cool. Mix the watercress and lovage or celery in a bowl. Whisk the olive oil into the cold vinegar mixture and pour over the greens. Sprinkle with salt and pepper and serve with sausages, cheese or slices of orange.

Spinning, weaving and dyeing

In ancient Greece all women took pride in their spinning and weaving. So when their king, Alexander the Great, defeated King Darius of Persia and took his queen captive, he gave her some wool and spindles to help pass the time. She was terribly insulted; in Persia this was slaves' work.

Before spinning, a sheep's fleece was first soaked in hot water to clean it and float off some of the grease. It was expensive to dye the wool at this stage because some wool would be lost when it was combed out. However if the wool was dyed now, any unevenness in colour disappeared when the wool was spun and woven (from this process we have the phrase 'dyed in the wool').

Spinning yarn

This woman holds a stick, called a distaff, with raw wool around it. She twisted and dropped her spindle, and as it spun, it pulled out the wool, twisting the fibres into yarn.

Weaving

Greek looms were made from heavy wooden beams and were set up permanently at home. In the picture you can see the rolled woven cloth at the top of the loom with the warp threads hanging down, tied and weighted with stones. The woman on the left pushes a line of weft with a stick, while her friend picks up some of the warp threads with a stick in one hand and pushes through her bobbin with the other.

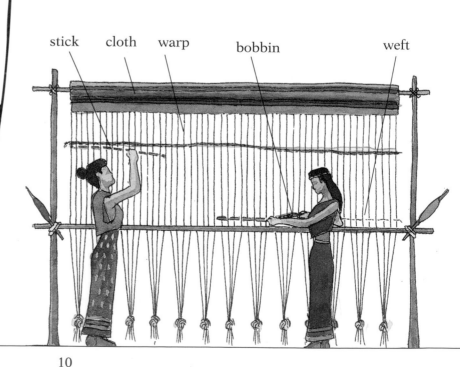

stick   cloth   warp   bobbin   weft

Dyeing

The Greeks made dyes from soaking various plants in hot water: stalks of weld (for yellow); roots of madder (for deep pink); oak bark (for brown) and fermented dried woad leaves (for blue). First the cloth was soaked in hot water with a handful of alum to stop the colour washing out. Then it was put in a dye vat, stirred gently for an hour to absorb the colour and rinsed in cold water.

dyeing vat

weld

dried balls
of woad

Making a netting bag

After the fleeces were sheared from the sheep they were collected in netting bags. To make your own netting bag you will need a ball of string.

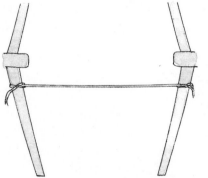

1 Tie a short piece of string between two chair legs to hold your netting firm. This is your base.

2 Now cut a longer piece of string and tie one end to the right hand edge of your base. Make a loop over your base string from the back. Make sure the loops are all the same size. Knot each loop loosely to the base string so it does not slip while you are working. Make six or seven more loops, tying them in each time. The last loop should be twice as long as the others.

Hold the last loop down with one finger while knotting the string through the end of the previous loop. Pull the knot tight, leave some string for a new loop, knot it again and so on, until the end of the line.

3 The new line is just the same except your knots are the other way around.

When you have finished, tie the end of the string tight to the last loop.

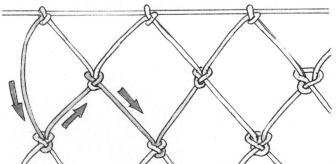

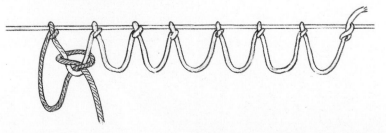

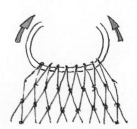

4 Run a piece of thick cord through the lines of loops at top and bottom and tie them to make a netting bag.

Preparing leather

After skinning an animal, the Greeks soaked the skin in a mixture of urine or pigeon dung and water to rot the outer layer. They then scraped off this fatty layer with its hair and sweat glands. The material that was left was called rawhide. They rubbed the rawhide with oil to soften it, but to make the softened skin waterproof it had to be tanned.

Tanning involved soaking the hide for weeks in a mixture of water and chips of oak bark. This produced leather which was then washed and dried, and rubbed with fish oil to soften it. No wonder the tanneries were all built on the east side of towns so that westerly winds would blow the smell away!

Leatherworkers

This shoemaker is working in his shop, with samples of his goods hanging above him. Leatherworkers used special knives with rounded blades so as not to pucker up the leather..

Greek sandals

You could make a similar pair of sandals to the ones this Ancient Greek woman is wearing.

Make a pair of Greek sandals

You will need a rectangle of paper for the pattern, two rectangles of leather or felt and two long strips for laces.

1 Using this diagram as your guide, stand on the paper and draw round one foot. The curved parts at toe and heel should be a little longer than your foot. The side flaps should almost meet over your foot. The ankle flaps should be wide enough for you to sew them together at the back. They should almost meet at the front.

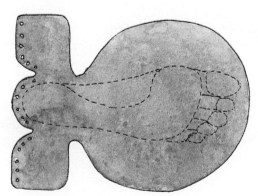

2 Lay your pieces of felt or leather face to face on the pattern and cut them both out together. This will make a right and left sandal. Carefully cut out loops in the ankle straps and pieces out of the side flaps.

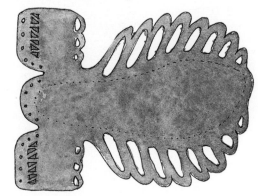

3 You don't have to follow this pattern exactly – just make sure the loops are not too thin. You can decorate the sandals with coloured paints, beads, or embroidery, if you want to. Sew up the back and lace your thongs through the loops. Tie the ends around your ankles.

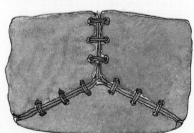

Homes and temples

The Greeks built their homes of bricks, made from mud mixed with chopped straw and dung, and dried in the sun. Because more rain fell in Greece than in other Mediterranean countries, they covered their roofs with terracotta tiles, which sloped down on both sides to allow the rain to run off. At the front they built a porch, supported by two wooden posts.

The Greeks built the first temples – special buildings to house the statues of their gods – in the same design as their houses, but with a row of wooden posts all the way round, a little way outside the walls. The roof was wider than the walls and rested on these posts, so it completely protected the walls. When they began to build in marble they did not need to protect the temple from rain, but they kept the same design, copying every detail in stone, even the wooden pegs that once held the beams together.

Building a Greek temple

Marble was carved into rough blocks at the quarry and hauled by oxen over a road of stone slabs, with deep grooves for the wheels.

The bent ends of the crane claws were pushed under the blocks. The claws were tied with rope to stop them opening.

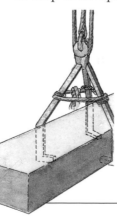

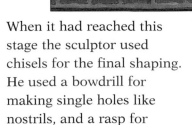

Carving a marble statue for a temple

It took between six to twelve months to carve a statue. Because marble was expensive, the sculptor had to plan each stage carefully, to avoid making mistakes.

First the sculptor drew a grid of squares all over the block of marble. Then he drew a figure on each side of the block, making sure, for example, that the knees were six squares up on each side. He used a punch and hammer to chip away the stone, working round the block.

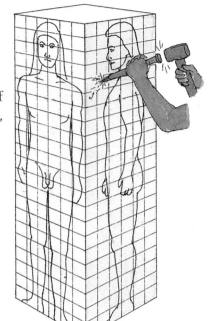

When it had reached this stage the sculptor used chisels for the final shaping. He used a bowdrill for making single holes like nostrils, and a rasp for smoothing the chisel marks.

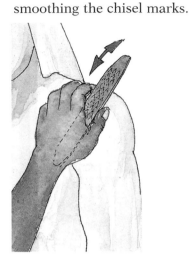

A stone block was lifted by cutting a hole with sloping sides and inserting three iron bars – the outside ones with small 'feet'. A rod slotted through holes in the bars was hooked to a crane.

The long lintels were lifted with crane and rope. It was difficult to position a lintel correctly, so sandbags were piled in the space between the columns. The lintel was placed across them and could be moved by letting sand out of the bags until it was in the correct position

15

Water, Heat, Light

In Greece, where summer rainfall was light and many rivers dried up, it was important to provide water for the townspeople. Special channels, or aqueducts, were built, lined with plaster and roofed with stone, to bring water to the public fountain from the hills, sometimes several kilometres away.

We do not know when one of the most important techniques of the ancient world – making charcoal – was discovered. Charcoal burns slowly without smoke, and can be quickly fanned to a higher temperature. It was ideal for cooking and heating in Greek houses which had no chimneys.

For lighting, the Greeks used little open clay lamps, filled with olive oil and with an oil-soaked wick hanging through the spout. Poor people might have to choose between having oil for lighting at night or for cooking. There was no streetlighting so people carried torches, made of sticks of pine smeared with pitch and tied with vine tendrils.

The public fountain

Women collecting water from the public fountain. The water vessels which they used for collecting the water had small handles on each side for carrying, and a large handle for pouring.

Supplying water

When the Greeks built aqueducts to supply water, they tunnelled straight through hills. There were good reasons for this. Going round the hill took longer and cost more. An outside channel might be destroyed by a landslide, or enemies might cut off the water supply. To build a tunnel, they first set posts up and over the hill, making sure they were in a straight line. Using a plumbline to keep the hole vertical, they dug shafts straight down. Then they dug into the sides of the hill from opposite ends to the shafts. Once they had reached these they used sighting rods, to keep in a straight line, meeting up with each shaft in turn.

shaft

lake

aqueduct

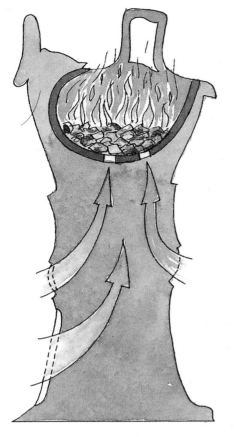

Heating and lighting homes

The charcoal in this portable stove was lit outside and brought in when it was glowing. The arrows show where the air comes in.

To light fires, countrypeople used a firedrill. This was a piece of wood with a hole filled with dried moss in which a stick of harder wood was twirled until it got so hot that the moss caught fire. Townspeople struck pieces of flint together, making sparks to set light to dry twigs.

This clay lampstand has spouts on either side, so it can hold three wicks.

Where to dig for a well

Try this experiment in summer. First look for sandy or fine gravelly soil, preferably near the foot of a hill. Be sure to tell an adult where you are going.

1 Go out at sunrise and lie face down on the ground. Look for signs of moisture rising. Check the plants nearby – bulrushes, alder, withy and ivy are good signs.

2 Dig a hole, smear olive oil inside a metal basin and put it upside down in your hole. Cover it with leaves and leave overnight.

3 If there are drops of water on the oil next day, you have found the right place to dig your well.

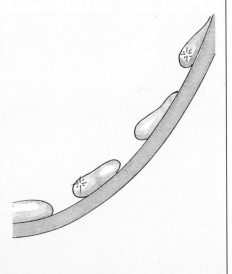

Crafts and Industry

Gold and silver

Silver paid for the Greek warships that defeated the Persians at the battle of Salamis in 480 BC. The slaves, who dug the silver from the mines, worked in low, narrow tunnels, dimly lit by oil lamps. There was very little ventilation and the slaves were always in danger of being poisoned by gases or crushed by collapsing tunnels.

The Greeks used gold and silver for coins, jewellery and decorating statues. Their favourite jewellery was plain gold, worked in complicated and delicate patterns.

Decorating statues

This statue, made in the fifth century BC, has silver teeth and eyelashes, copper lips and glass eyes.

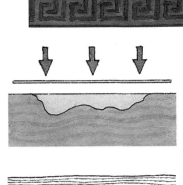

Making gold earrings

These earrings were made in about 425 BC. To make the main, boat-shaped part, the goldsmith beat a lump of gold into a thin sheet. The shape was then cut out and pressed into a wooden die.

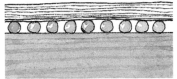

To make the decoration of tiny gold balls, the goldsmith hcatcd little pieces of gold. They were laid in a pattern on glue-covered papyrus, painted with copper and a sheet of gold was glued over them. This 'sandwich' was turned over, wetted and the papyrus peeled off. When heated in a kiln, the balls stuck to their gold base.

The pendants, shaped like tiny shells, were made in two halves. A thin piece of gold was laid between the moulded end of a bronze stamp and a piece of beeswax or lead, and hammered with a wooden mallet.

How to make Greek chain jewellery

To make the chain you will need some strong silver foil and glue.
Or you could use thin wire, twisting the ends together to make loops.

1 Cut some long, narrow strips of foil about 5 mm wide. Twist each strip until it is folded all the way along, then roll it between your hands until it looks like round wire. Now cut your 'wire' into pieces of the same length. The longer you make them the bigger your loops will be. Glue each piece together to make a loop.

2 Curl each loop round into a U-shape. To make a single chain, thread each loop through the one before. Tie the ends together when it is long enough.

3 To make a double loop, thread each new loop through the ends of the two previous loops. This makes a prettier chain, especially if you use different coloured foil or wire loops.

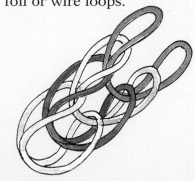

Bronze and iron

Around 3000 BC metalworkers in Syria discovered that if they added tin to copper ore before they heated it to melt out the metal, it produced a much more useful mixture – bronze. Melted bronze was runnier than copper and easier to pour into moulds. When bronze cooled it was harder and better for tools. The metalworkers began to experiment, trying different mixtures. More tin made the bronze white and brittle, less tin made it tougher.

The Greeks could not get their fires hot enough to melt iron. They piled the ore in a furnace, but what they found after the fire had died down was lumps of iron mixed with cinder and ash, which had to be hammered out. Then they heated and hammered it over and over again. Allowing it to cool slowly produced iron.

Metalworking

The blacksmith is heating a bar of iron, holding it in his tongs. Working with iron needed a very hot fire and the blacksmith's assistant is using a pair of bellows to heat up the furnace. The bellows were big bags made of oxskin, each with a clay pipe leading into the furnace.

Making a bronze statue

Until about 525 BC the Greeks carved their statues in marble. When they began to cast their statues in bronze they found it less brittle than marble, so they could make figures in more interesting poses, such as holding out their arms.

1 To cast a statue the sculptor first covered a wooden core with clay, in the rough shape required.

2 This was covered with melted beeswax, which was carved and smoothed into the exact shape wanted. Now a layer of fine clay was smoothed over the beeswax, and worked into all the corners. It had to be perfect as this layer was the mould of the outside of the statue. Bronze pins were pushed through into the core to hold the mould in place.

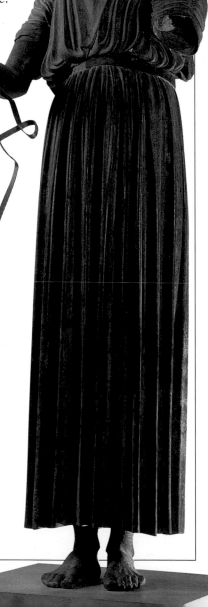

3 When the mould was dry, it was placed in a kiln (oven) to fire the clay and melt out the wax. Then the mould was put in a pit and tightly packed with earth to support the clay when the melted bronze was poured in.

4 The sculptor's assistants heated the bronze to over 1,000°C, poured it into the top of the mould with funnels and left it to cool. Now came the moment of truth. Crowds came to watch the clay coat being broken away from a big statue and see the sculptor polishing and engraving the final details.

21

Pottery

Clay was cheap and the Greeks used it to make everything they possibly could. They used it for cooking stoves, ladles, babies' high chairs and pots big enough to bathe in or small enough to drink from. The Greeks were lucky to have good red clay, containing iron, but it was their technology which made their pottery the best in the ancient world.

The potter's wheel

This vase painting shows a Greek potter in about 500 BC, sitting at his wheel and working it with his foot.

Potters worked in four stages: preparing the clay, shaping it on the wheel, decorating the pot and firing it in the kiln. Each time they thought of a new idea for one stage, it affected other stages. When they invented a faster wheel, they needed smoother clay. They mixed freshly-dug clay with water and when the grit sank, they filtered off the finer clay, leaving it to dry out until it was thick enough to model.

The development of the wheel

1. The first wheel was a heavy wooden disc which spun on a stone base.

2. Later the work surface was raised to make the turning wheel bigger and heavier.

3. Around 550 to 500 BC the work surface was raised so high that the potter could sit upright and push the flywheel with his foot. The smoother clay he now used meant he could half-dry his pot, turn it upside down on the wheel and scrape the sides to make them thinner.

Decorating the pots

The potter decorated his pot by drawing the outline of his picture with a pointed stick on the slightly damp surface. Then he mixed very fine red clay, water and wood ash to form a thin red jelly. With this he painted the parts he wanted to go black. He painted the white decoration with a mixture of white clay and water.

When Greek potters first invented their method of firing, they left the background red and painted figures in the jelly-like paint that turned black in the kiln. If they wanted red details on the figures they had to scratch lines through the paint. Later they realized that it was more effective to leave the figures red and paint the background black.

Firing the pots

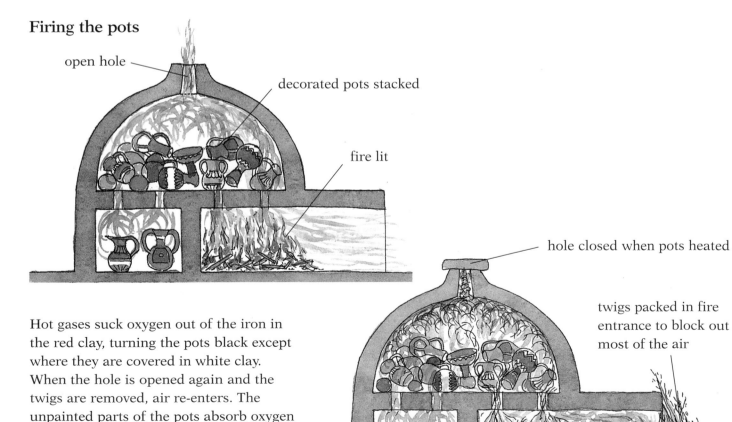

open hole

decorated pots stacked

fire lit

hole closed when pots heated

twigs packed in fire entrance to block out most of the air

Hot gases suck oxygen out of the iron in the red clay, turning the pots black except where they are covered in white clay. When the hole is opened again and the twigs are removed, air re-enters. The unpainted parts of the pots absorb oxygen from the air and turn red again – the painted parts stay black.

Glassworking

A coloured glass bowl

This bowl was made in the second century BC, after the Greeks had discovered how to produce clear glass. They saw how beautiful clear and coloured glass looked when used together.

The earliest glassmakers, the Mesopotamians (who lived in the region that is now Iraq) valued glass because it could be brightly coloured with minerals to look like semi-precious stones such as turquoise, blue lapis lazuli and golden cornelian. The Mesopotamians discovered how to make glass by melting together soda, lime and sand. At first they ground the cooled glass into the shape they wanted. It took some time to work out how to handle glass while it was still hot and runny.

The Greeks probably imported pieces of raw coloured glass from Syria and Palestine and turned them into jewellery, bowls and little jars for perfumed oils in their workshops. Glass was expensive because shaping it took a long time and a lot of skill.

Making a glass mosaic bowl

1 The glassmaker made the mosaic sections by coating white glass with melted clear glass and stretching it to form ribbons. He coated the ribbons with melted coloured glass and rolled them up.

2 When the rolls cooled he cut them into slices and laid them into the shape of the bowl. He heated the slices until they melted and stuck together.

3 He heated and softened the bowl, draped it over a mould and put it into the kiln. As the glass softened it sagged over the mould which is why this method is called sagging or slumping.

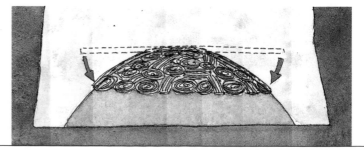

Glass necklaces

Glass bead necklaces like this were popular with women and men in Crete in about 1300 BC. The Cretans imported blocks of blue glass from Egypt, melted them and poured the hot, soft glass into baked clay moulds.

How to make a necklace

You will need plasticine (the Greeks used beeswax), plaster of Paris, modelling clay, dark blue paint and varnish.

1 Make a model of your bead by shaping a rectangle from plasticine, 1.5 cm by 1.0 cm and 0.6 cm thick. Decorate the surface with a pattern of raised lines and circles.

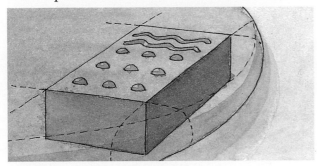

2 Now make your plaster mould. Lay the model face upwards on waxed paper and build a pasticine wall around it 3 cm high. Mix up plaster of Paris and pour it in, filling the wall up to the top. Leave it to set.

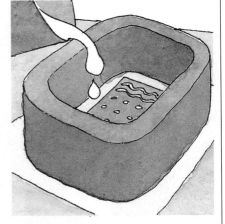

3 When the plaster has set, take off all the plasticine and the paper. Your bead-shaped mould is ready.

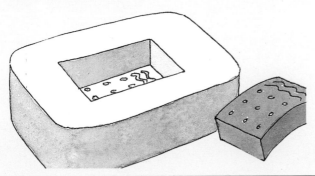

4 Press some modelling clay into the mould, smooth it off and let it dry until it is hard enough to take out. With a thick needle, push a hole through the bead for your thread. When your bead is dry, paint it dark blue (to look like lapis lazuli) and give it a coat of varnish.

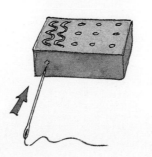

Painting and decoration

Decorating walls

This fresco of a tropical landscape is from the palace at Knossos in Crete. Fresco painting is permanent because the paint becomes part of the plaster. The artist put two layers of plaster on the wall, then drew the outline of his picture over the whole wall. He put a third layer of plaster over a small area, quickly redrew the outline, and while the plaster was still wet, painted on pigment mixed with water. He had to work fast because the pigment would not bond properly to dry plaster.

The Ancient Greeks loved colour. The paint has worn off their marble temples, tombstones and statues, but when they were new they glowed with colour. The clothes of the carved gods around the tops of temples were painted in bright colours to contrast with their skin.

The Greeks mixed paints in different ways, according to what they were decorating. They decorated the walls of their houses using tempera paints or fresco painting. To make tempera the Greeks ground pigments into powder, mixing in a little honey (to stop the paint drying) and lightly beaten egg white (to make it stick). They also used a technique called encaustic painting, which did not wash off.

Making pigments

The Greeks made pigments (colours) from ground-up roots, leaves and mineral ores. Woad made blue, sand and copper ore made a deeper blue, madder roots made rose, copper ore made green, chalk or white lead made white, soot made black.

Encaustic painting

The artist used encaustic paint for this picture painted on a wooden coffin. Pigments were mixed with beeswax and resin and put into bronze saucers. They were kept hot and runny over a charcoal stove. A wooden panel was covered with a coat of tempera paint. Then the artist laid on the encaustic colours (in the saucers) with a flat knife, building up layers of lighter and darker paint. Finally, the finished painting was held over a stove, warming it just enough for all the colours to merge slightly, without running and spoiling the picture.

Make an encaustic painting

You could follow this method of painting, mixing wax crayons with grated candle wax and warming the mixture over a radiator. Your picture will have a bright, slightly transparent look.

Health

Treating the sick

Although Greek doctors were skilful in dealing with injuries, they did not understand the causes of diseases. Medicine was a mixture of science and religion. Sick people might visit the shrine of Asclepius, the god of medicine and healing. They would pray and rest there, waiting for the god to come to them in a dream and heal them.

Hippocrates was born in 460 BC. He is called 'the father of medicine' because he was the first to treat medicine as a science, observing all the patient's symptoms and taking careful notes. He realized that diseases come from natural causes; for instance that wounds left open to the air become infected, and that stagnant water is harmful, although he did not understand the reasons why. He also realized that the human body has natural defences that fight disease, and that it was the doctor's job to help the body to heal itself.

Setting bones

Hippocrates used this table in about 420 BC to reset dislocated joints and to pull the ends of broken bones into place so they could be splinted. The patient was laid on the table. Ropes were tied to the body and wound round drums at one end of the table, and to the end of the broken limb and around drums at the other end. Helpers at each end turned the drums with handles, pulling the patient until the bone ends were in the right place.

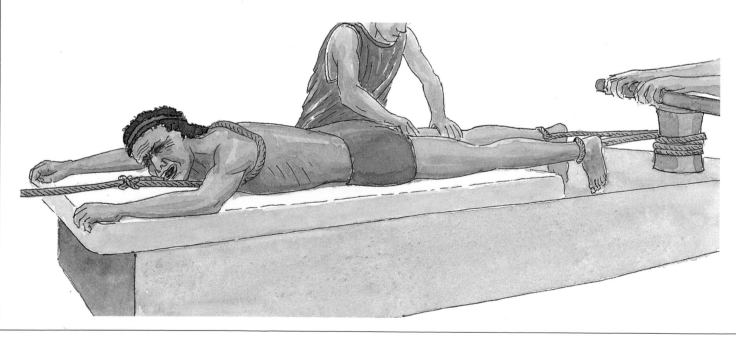

Cupping a patient

Hippocrates believed that the body is a balance of four 'humours', which consisted of blood, phlegm, black bile and yellow bile. Too much of any of these could cause illness. Here the doctor is drawing blood from the patient by cupping. He made a cut in the patient's arm and the bowl, containing a burning cloth, was pressed over the cut. This created a vacuum and caused blood to be drawn out into the cup.

Medical instuments

These instruments were made by casting bronze (see page 21), then hammering into shape and heating to restore their spring. Then they were dipped in water to harden them. Needles were made as long strips. They were sharpened at each end and cut in half.

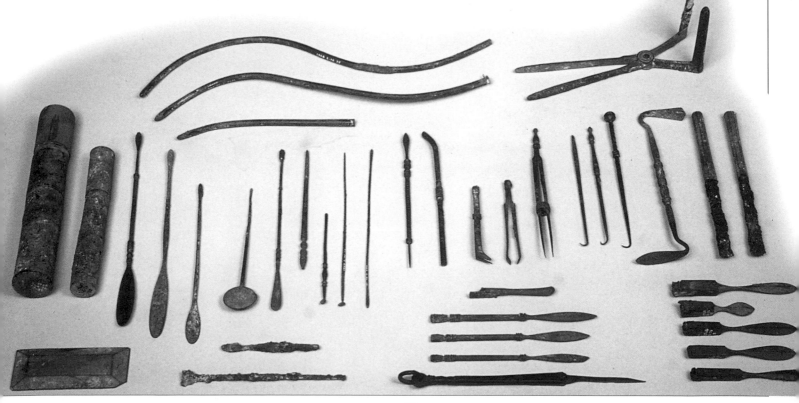

Cosmetics and perfumes

One of the things we might miss most if we lived in Ancient Greece would be a daily bath or shower. There was no running water or soap. After exercising at the gymnasium, men cleaned themselves by rubbing olive oil onto their skin, scraping it off with a strigil and rinsing in cold water. Women washed themselves with a bowl of water and a cloth.

Greek women used white lead or ground chalk as face powder. Although the lead was poisonous and sometimes caused their deaths, it was very popular. Chalk was safer but it washed off easily. After putting on face powder, women applied rouge, made of mulberry juice or ground red seaweed. Joined-up eyebrows were a sign of a sexy character, so they filled up the space between their eyes and drew lines around their eyes, using soot made from burnt powdered rose leaves mixed with water and gum.

Cleaning the skin

A bottle for olive oil for rubbing into the skin, and strigils for scraping the oil off.

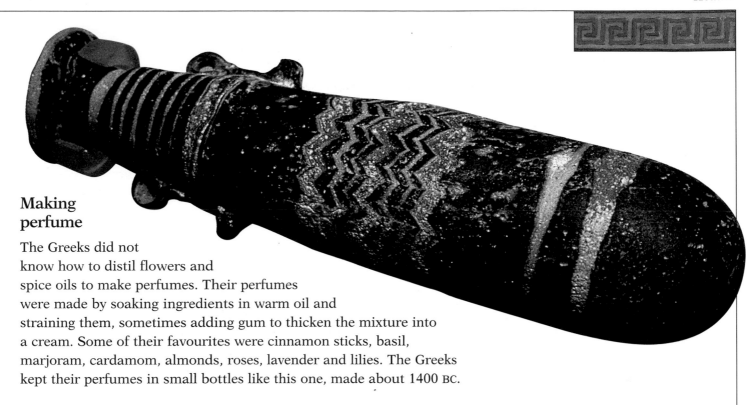

Making perfume

The Greeks did not
know how to distil flowers and
spice oils to make perfumes. Their perfumes
were made by soaking ingredients in warm oil and
straining them, sometimes adding gum to thicken the mixture into
a cream. Some of their favourites were cinnamon sticks, basil,
marjoram, cardamom, almonds, roses, lavender and lilies. The Greeks
kept their perfumes in small bottles like this one, made about 1400 BC.

How to make perfume

You could make dry perfume or perfumed oil
using some of these ingredients

1 Pick flowerpetals and leaves
in the morning and spread
them in a warm, dark place
until dry. When dry, grind each
ingredient separately. The
Greeks used a pestle and mortar
– you could use an electric
grinder.

2 Now pour the mixture into a
jar, close it tightly and leave
in a dark place for a few days
for the smells to mix. If you find
one smell is too strong, add
more of something else and
leave it for a while. You could
put the dry perfume into a little
cloth bag and hang it in your
wardrobe.

3 To make perfumed oil, fill a
glass jar with a mixture of
freshly picked flowers, leaves
and crushed spices, fill it up
with cooking oil, screw on the
top and leave it on a sunny
windowsill for a fortnight,
shaking it well every day.
Then strain off the oil.

Land travel

The Greeks did not bother much with building roads. One reason was the high cost of road-building in such mountainous countryside. And roads were not really necessary because no-one lived far from the main town. Farmers could easily take their produce to market by mule and if they needed to travel further it was far quicker to go by boat.

Roads were mostly tracks, dusty in summer and wet and muddy in winter. If the Greeks needed a good road, for a special reason, they laid stone slabs with deep grooves for wheels to run in (see page 14). One road like this ran across the Isthmus of Corinth (near the modern Corinth canal). The sailors loaded their ships on to trolleys and pulled them along the road from one side of the isthmus to the other.

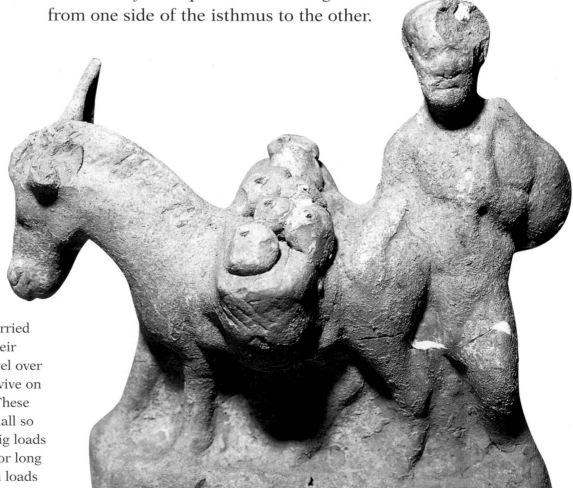

Donkey and mule transport

Donkeys and mules carried panniers slung over their backs. They could travel over rough ground and survive on little food and water. These animals were quite small so they could not carry big loads and were best suited for long journeys with smallish loads over rough ground.

Ox transport

Oxen pull with power from their shoulders and can haul heavily laden carts. They are sure-footed but slow. Because of their slowness the Greeks used them mainly for pulling heavy loads over shortish distances. The first carts were designed to be pulled by oxen and for them the yoke and pole worked well. The yoke sat in front of the ox's hump, with straps round its throat and stomach to stop it slipping up. Because of the power in its shoulders, the ox pushes up on the yoke to haul its load.

Horse transport

Horses were used for pulling lightweight chariots carrying passengers. A horse's power comes from its hind legs. Because it has no hump, when a horse pulls on a heavy load the yoke slides back, the straps tighten around its long neck and squeeze its windpipe. Why didn't the Greeks invent a better harness for horses? Probably because they had no need to – their harness worked well enough for pulling light chariots.

Travel by sea

The people living around the Mediterranean have traded with each other across the sea for thousands of years. The Greeks found it was better to carry goods around the coast rather than overland through the mountains. When they wanted to build a town they always checked that there was a good anchorage nearby.

There were no passenger ships in the Mediterranean. Anyone wanting to travel would pack food and a tent, find a cargo boat going in the right direction and bargain with the captain for a space on deck. There were no lifeboats; if the ship was in danger, passengers would tie valuables around their neck so whoever found the body would think themselves paid well enough to bury it properly.

Greek ships

This vase painting shows the difference between the fat, heavy trading ship, which the Greeks called a 'round ship', and the long, narrow, low trireme which they called a 'long ship'. (see page 38).

An early ship

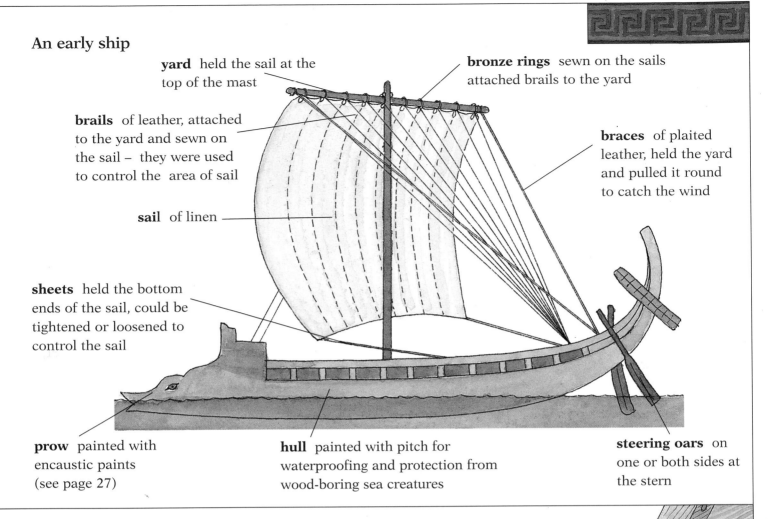

yard held the sail at the top of the mast

brails of leather, attached to the yard and sewn on the sail – they were used to control the area of sail

sail of linen

sheets held the bottom ends of the sail, could be tightened or loosened to control the sail

bronze rings sewn on the sails attached brails to the yard

braces of plaited leather, held the yard and pulled it round to catch the wind

prow painted with encaustic paints (see page 27)

hull painted with pitch for waterproofing and protection from wood-boring sea creatures

steering oars on one or both sides at the stern

Building a hull

The shipbuilder laid down a long, thick plank for the keel and fixed the stem and sternposts to it. He carved the planks for the hull and fixed them together edge-to-edge using mortice and tenon joints.

Then he carved curved rib planks and fixed them to the inside of the hull by boring a hole from the outside into the rib, hammering in a wooden dowel and into that an iron nail.

rib planks

dowel

deck

rib

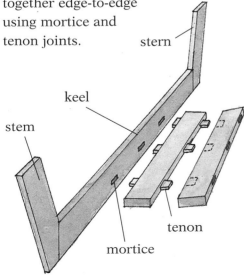

stern

keel

stem

tenon

mortice

Long planks running from stem to stern on top of the ribs made a strong base for the cargo. Finally the shipbuilder fitted the deck and steering oars and painted the seams with pitch and beeswax.

Hoplites and weapons

In Ancient Greece, when soldiers were needed, citizens offered their services, bringing whatever weapons they had. Poor farmers brought hunting slings and bows. Men who could afford armour became hoplites, the main part of the army. Hoplites made a wall of shields, pushing forward, stabbing with their long spears.

The best long-range weapon the Greeks had in 500 BC was the composite bow, which fired an arrow about 260 m. The only way to shoot further was to make the bow stiffer and this meant a new way of drawing the bow. They invented two different versions. One kept the basic bow shape. The other was a new design, a catapult. With these they could fire heavy iron bolts or stone shots.

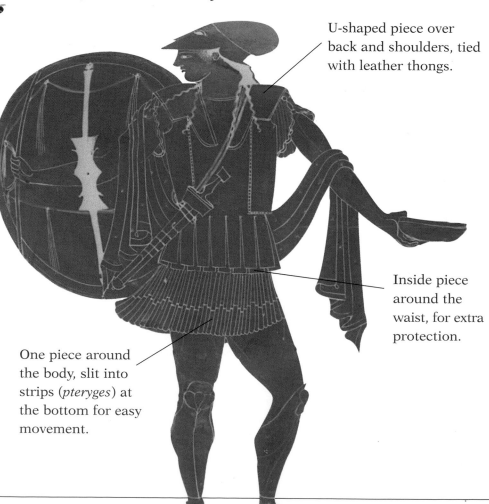

U-shaped piece over back and shoulders, tied with leather thongs.

Armour

A hoplite wore a bronze helmet and leg guards. He carried a bronze shield on his left arm. In his right hand he carried an iron-tipped spear or an iron sword.

The cuirass

Most hoplites wore a linen cuirass, which was just as efficent and lighter and cheaper than bronze. The armourer cut the linen cuirass in three pieces. To make the cuirass as thick as possible, he cut about ten of each piece and glued them together.

One piece around the body, slit into strips (*pteryges*) at the bottom for easy movement.

Inside piece around the waist, for extra protection.

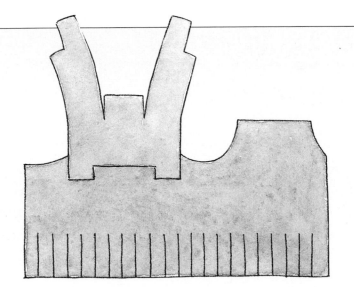

To make a cuirass

You could make a cuirass using some stiff material. Canvas or a thick curtain would do. Cut out and sew the material using this pattern. Cut strips along the bottom for the *pteryges*.

The crossbow or 'belly-shooter'

To cock the bow, the archer rested the diostra against a wall, pressing the curved bar with his stomach, forcing back the diostra and bowstring

Archer placed iron bolt in slot and into notch at end of bolt, pulled back lever – claw released the bowstring.

Bow made of horn, wood and sinew.

Diostra, with slot along top to take bolt, slid back and forth in groove in lower piece of wood.

Two-pronged iron claw with pin held bowstring when diostra was pushed forward.

Wooden pawl caught in metal teeth to stop diostra sliding forward.

Lever under claw held bowstring until archer took aim.

The catapult

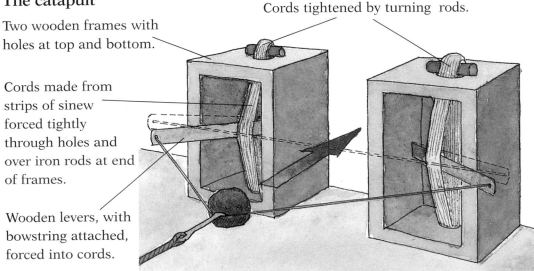

Two wooden frames with holes at top and bottom.

Cords made from strips of sinew forced tightly through holes and over iron rods at end of frames.

Wooden levers, with bowstring attached, forced into cords.

Cords tightened by turning rods.

When the drawstring was drawn back by a windlass, it pulled on the levers forcing the ends together, twisting and tightening the cords.

As the drawstring was released, the levers swung back with terrific pressure, projecting the missile forward.

The ship as a weapon

By about 2500 BC two main kinds of ships were being built around the Mediterranean: fat, heavy sailing ships for carrying goods and light, fast galleys for moving people. The fast galley became the warship. A raised deck was added to carry soldiers, who attacked enemy ships with bows, javelins and grappling hooks.

The Greeks turned the warship into a weapon – a battering ram on water. Their light, narrow boat was tipped with a heavy bronze ram which they rowed straight at the enemy ship. The aim was to smash a hole in its side underwater and make a quick getaway.

To do this the Greeks had to solve several technical problems. Their ship had to ram the enemy very fast. If they hit slowly their own ship would crumple, leaving the enemy unhurt. They found that longer oars gave more speed, but to fit them they had to make the ship wider, which slowed it down. Using more oarsmen made the ship too long and unable to turn quickly. Putting extra oarsmen in a row above the others made the ship top-heavy so it capsized easily. Their answer to all these problems was the special arrangement of rowers' seats in what they called the trireme.

Trireme

Every part of the trireme was designed to make it as fast and light as possible.

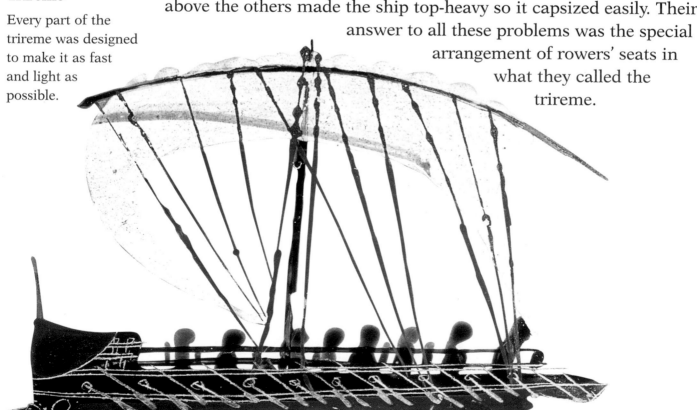

The trireme

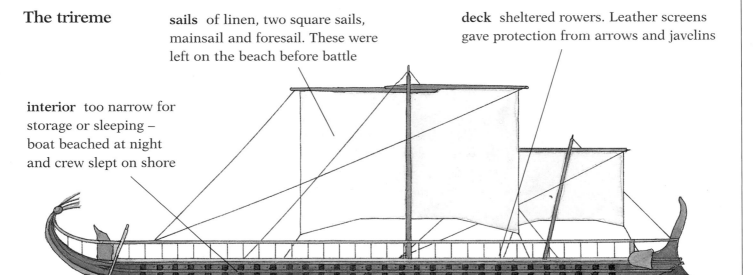

sails of linen, two square sails, mainsail and foresail. These were left on the beach before battle

deck sheltered rowers. Leather screens gave protection from arrows and javelins

interior too narrow for storage or sleeping – boat beached at night and crew slept on shore

hull of pine for lightness. Length 35 m, width 3.7 m, height above waterline 2.5 m and below water 1 m

oars 4.3 m in length except for a few slightly shorter at bow and stern. Oarsmen rested oars against wooden pins with leather thongs to stop them slipping

ram square-tipped and made of bronze

The oarsmen

At the top, outside and slightly higher than the second level sat the *thranites*, who worked their oars with an outrigger. A *thranite's* oar went into the sea between those of the *thalamite* and *zygite*. The *thranite* was the only one who could see the end of his oar so he could adjust his stroke to keep time with the other two. His job was the hardest because his oar was the most upright. There were 31 oarsmen in the top row, 27 in each of the other rows.

Below, on the second level were the *zygites*, who rowed over the side.

The lowest level of rowers, called *thalamites* (meaning in the hold) could not see out. Their oars poked through portholes about 40 cm above sea level, with a leather bag around the oar to keep the sea out of the ship.

Writing and signalling messages

What people used to write on depended on what they needed the writing for. The Ancient Greeks enjoyed reading and writing, so it is not surprising they used a lot of different writing materials. Permanent records, like the laws of a city, were inscribed on bronze tablets.

Bronze was fine for public records, but not very practical to read at home after supper, and by 500 BC so many people were wanting copies of plays, poems, history books, or speeches by famous politicians, that there was a regular book market in Athens. These books were made of sheets of papyrus imported from Egypt. They were copied in Greek workshops and glued into rolls.

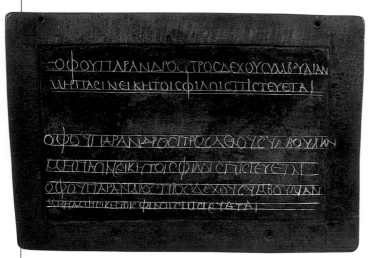

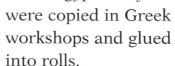

Writing tablets

Small wooden tablets, with a layer of beeswax mixed with soot, were ideal for writing letters. The person receiving a tablet smoothed over the message, wrote their reply and returned it. This tablet belonged to a schoolchild. Can you tell which is the teacher's writing and which the pupil's copy?

The Greeks wrote on wax tablets with a stylus made of bronze, bone or silver. This terracotta model shows a boy writing with a stylus on a wax tablet.

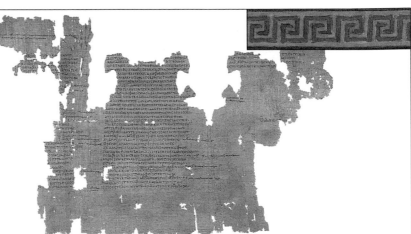

Papyrus sheets

Papyrus sheets were rolled round a wooden rod. The Greeks wrote in columns. To read the papyrus, the Greeks held the rod in their right hand and pulled it out with their left hand. When they finished, they rolled the papyrus back. To write on papyrus sheets, they used a reed, sharpened at one end and ink made from soot mixed with water.

Signalling over a distance

Ancient peoples sent signals by lighting fires on hilltops. The problem was they could only send one pre-arranged message. In 350 BC, Aeneas, a Trojan prince, invented a way of sending several different messages.

1 To use Aeneas' signalling method you need two tall containers with holes and stoppers at the bottom, two sticks and two corks smaller than the necks of the containers. Draw lines three finger-breadths apart on the sticks and number them. Each line means a different message.

2 Push the sticks into the corks. Fill the containers with water and put the corks in so they float with the sticks upright.

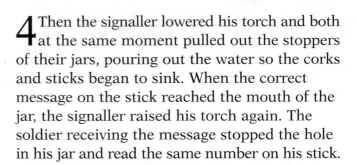

3 Greek soldiers signalled to each other by taking a jar and torch to a hilltop. When one wanted to send a message he lit his torch and raised it until the other noticed and raised his own torch.

4 Then the signaller lowered his torch and both at the same moment pulled out the stoppers of their jars, pouring out the water so the corks and sticks began to sink. When the correct message on the stick reached the mouth of the jar, the signaller raised his torch again. The soldier receiving the message stopped the hole in his jar and read the same number on his stick.

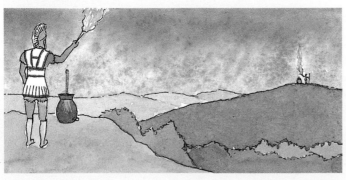

Sports and Music

Music was very important to Greek athletes. They often exercised to music and at the Olympic Games a piper played for long jumpers and discus throwers to help them get the right rhythm.

The Greeks were probably the first people to use sports equipment – boxing gloves, discuses and weights. Their main musical instruments were the lyre and the pipes. They thought the lyre was invented by the god Hermes, and the goddess Athena first played the pipes, but she threw them away because they made her cheeks puff out! Girls played drums and clicked castanets to keep time while they danced.

Musical instruments

The lyre was a wooden frame with strings, made of gut (from animal intestines). The strings were wound round pegs at the top so they could be tightened. A hollow sounding box at the bottom made the sound louder.

The Olympic Games

A long-jumper jumped with his weights from a standing position, swinging the weights forward to pull him forward. He needed split-second timing to land on his feet.

Boxing

Boxers fought fiercely, sometimes for hours until one gave in. These boxers are wearing fingerless leather gloves with thick leather straps around the knuckles.

Olympic rewards

After the Olympic Games, each competition winner received a wreath made from branches of the sacred olive tree which grew behind the Temple of Zeus. He was also given woollen fillets (tokens) to bind round his head and arms.

To make Olympic fillets, you need four strands of wool. Cut each strand twice the length of the fillet you want. Knot the strands at one end and fix the knot to a table with a drawing pin.

1 Loop each strand over a pencil. Push the loops together.

2 Hold the strands firmly with one hand and, starting from the left, weave strand A under B, over C, and under D. Lay the end over the pencil to keep it out of the way for the moment. Now weave strand B under C, over D and under A (bring down strand A in a line with the others first). Lay strand B over pencil to keep it tidy. Carry on with strand C, then D, then A again and so on, until you have used up all the wool.

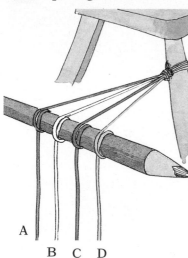

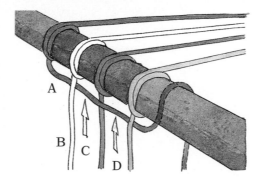

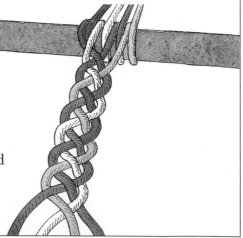

3 Check the edge as you go – if either side is pulled or left loose, your braid will start to curve. When you have finished, slide it off the pencil and knot each end to stop it unravelling.

Technology through Time

6000 BC	Pieces of the volcanic rock obsidian found on the mainland prove that the Greeks were capable of reaching the island of Melos by boat, to trade.
1600–1200 BC	Remains of a beam-press for pressing olives found on the island of Theresia.
1400–1200 BC	Mycenean glassworkers import ingots of raw blue glass from Egypt and melt them in moulds to make beads and ornaments.
1200–800 BC	Collapse of the Mycenean civilization. Art of writing disappears. Very little is known about this period except that the knowledge of ironwork appears.
770 BC	A new alphabet is borrowed from the Phoenicians and added to suit the Greek language.
750 BC	First evidence of forming glass bowls by slumping them over moulds in Phoenicia. This method later used in Greece.
700–600 BC	Mesopotamian glassworkers settle on the island of Rhodes, setting up workshops to make core-formed glass containers for perfumes and scented creams made on the island.
c.650 BC	The first life-size marble statues carved.
650–600 BC	The first large bronze statues made by the lost-wax method.
	The first coins made in the Greek cities of Ionia. Design only on one side.
600 BC	Open-cast mining for silver begun.
600–590 BC	Invention of the modern shape of the anchor that would not drag in heavy seas.
	By this time there was general use of iron tools, rather than tools made of stone or bronze.
500 BC	The first coins with designs stamped on both sides.
500–485 BC	The Treasury at Delphi – built entirely of marble.

500–400 BC	Grain-rubbers for grinding wheat used.
	Clear glass used for eyes and decorations on statues.
	Book trade becomes organized; books (papyrus scrolls) of literature, philosophy and speeches are manufactured and sold.
447–440	The Parthenon built.
BC430–440 BC	Appollodorus mixes colours and uses shadows and perspective in paintings – the first Greek artist to do so.
420 BC	Hippocrates invents the first operating table for setting dislocated and broken limbs.
400 BC	The 'belly-shooter' (a type of crossbow) is invented.
400–370 BC	Pamphilos and his pupil Pausias of Sikya develop the technique of encaustic painting.
350 BC	Development of a catapult powered by two torsion springs.
300–250 BC	Evidence of large plates and bowls made of mosaic glass and sandwich glass made in the Greek settlement of Canosa in southern Italy.
300–250 BC	Rotary handmills for grinding grain used.
250–200 BC	The 'Archimedean' screw-pump for raising water, possibly designed by Archimedes, in use.
250–200 BC	During the siege of Syracuse, cranes designed by Archimedes used to capsize enemy ships.
200 BC	Screwpress used for pressing olives and grapes.

Glossary

Anchorage A sheltered place where ships can anchor, protected from storms.

Archaeologists People who study objects from ancient times.

Charcoal Fuel made by partly burnt wood. It burns at a higher temperature than wood and was vital for metalworking.

Cuirass Armour that covered the chest and back.

Die A shaped tool used to design and cut metal.

Dislocated When a limb is put out of joint.

Distaff A rod on which thread is wound before spinning.

Distil To purify a liquid by first turning it into vapour by heat and back into a liquid by cooling.

Furnace A type of large oven in which great heat can be produced.

Gum The sticky fluid from the bark of acacia trees.

Hoplites Heavily armed Greek foot-soldiers.

Import To bring goods into a country.

Isthmus A narrow neck of land joining two larger land areas.

Kiln A large oven used for firing (baking) pottery and bricks.

Lintels Timber or stone supports over doorways or windows.

Mosaic A design made with small pieces of coloured glass.

Mould A shape into which a liquid substance is poured, so that the substance takes the same shape when cooled.

Ore Rock which contains metals combined with other chemicals.

Papyrus Paper used by the Greeks, made from the stem of the papyrus plant.

Philosopher Someone who thinks deeply about the basic laws of the universe and the principles of human behaviour.

Pitch The sticky black substance that runs from pine wood when it is piled up, covered with damp earth and slowly burnt.

Plumbline A string weighted with lead, which hangs vertically to measure that height or depth is straight.

Resin The sticky fluid which flows from the bark of fir and pine trees.

Rotary mill A machine for grinding corn, where the upper millstone could be turned round and round by hand.

Sickle A tool with a sharp curved blade, used for cutting grain.

Spindle A thin rod with a notch in it, used to draw out fibres for spinning into thread.

Stylus A pointed instrument used for writing on wax tablets.

Tanning The process of turning animal skin into leather.

Terracotta The word means 'red earth'. It describes the colour of the clay used by the Greeks to make their pottery.

Vacuum A space from which air and gas has been removed.

Warp In weaving, the threads that are stretched lengthwise across the loom.

Weft The threads that are passed across the loom, under and over the warp threads,

Windlass A machine used for raising weights by turning a handle to wind a rope around a drum.

Further information

Books to read

Craft Topics: Greeks by R Wright (Franklin Watts, l994)

Eyewitness Guides: Ancient Greece by Anita Ganeri (Dorling Kindersley, 1993)

History as Evidence: Ancient Greece by John Ellis Jones (Kingfisher, 1992)

I Was There: Ancient Greece by J D Clare (Riverswift, 1994)

Look Into the Past: The Greeks by A Susan Williams (Wayland, 1993)

The Original Olympics by Stewart Ross (Wayland, 1996)

CD Rom

Ancient Lands (Microsoft)

Places to visit

The British Museum, London. The Museum has a large collection of Greek vases, statues and artefacts.

Hadrian's Wall, in Northumberland and Cumbria

Roman Baths Museum, Bath

The National Museum in Athens has a superb collection of statues, vases and other Greek artefacts.

There are many marvellous examples of the ancient Greek civilization in countries around the Mediterranean, particularly on mainland Greece and the Greek islands.

Picture acknowledgements

The pictures in this book were supplied by: AKG London 6, 9, 13, 21, 22, 29(top), 40(right), 43(left); Ancient Art and Architecture Collection title page, 5, 7, 8, 10, 15, 16, 17, 18, 19, 20, 24, 25, 31, 32, 34; National Archaeological Museum, Athens/Bridgeman Art Library 26; British Library 40(left), 41; British Museum 27(lower); Judith Crosher 11(all), 27(top); C. M. Dixon cover, 36(top); Michael Holford 38, 42(right), 43; Wayland Picture Library 12, 23, 29(lower), 30, 33, 36(lower), 44-5 (all). Cover artwork Christa Hook, cover logo John Yates.

Index

Page numbers in **bold** indicate that there is information about the subject in a photograph or diagram.